The Latest:

20 Ghazals for 2020

Cover art: Kirsten Deirup
Best Wishes, 2023
Oil on linen
22 x 26 inches
55.9 x 66 cm
Courtesy of the artist and HESSE FLATOW, New York
Photo: Jenny Gorman

Cover design: Brianna Protesto
Interior design: Claire Eder
Publisher: Allison Blevins
Director: Kristiane Weeks-Rogers

THE LATEST: 20 GHAZALS FOR 2020
DENISE DUHAMEL, JULIE MARIE WADE
ISBN 978-1-957248-42-4
Harbor Editions,
an imprint of Small Harbor Publishing

The Latest:

20 Ghazals for 2020

Denise Duhamel & Julie Marie Wade

Harbor Editions
Small Harbor Publishing

For Maureen Seaton
(1947—2023)

Contents

The Latest:

20 Ghazals for 2020

Now Friend, the Belovèd has stolen your words—
Read slowly: The plot will unfold in real time.

— Agha Shahid Ali

Nostalgic Ghazal

Remember the good old days of dining out,
no masks or wipes at the Publix checkout?

Remember the sweet recent past of shared
bags of chips, picnics where we'd pig out

on zesty gherkins and warm buttered rolls?
Now America is sent to her room, a timeout

for trash-talking and unscrupulous PDA.
We grow paunchy, no gyms to work out;

our President, a fathead who feasts
on lies and KFC, fears healthy voter turnout.

Remember when we didn't need CBD
to sleep? To watch CNN without freaking out?

Remember when our worst fears were figments
of the future? Now, the future's here. Look out

for murder hornets and unmasked men droning
on about hoaxes, militia with their bug-out

bags lurking and looting at Black Lives Matter
protests, smashing store windows, then slipping out

to call the cops on Antifa. Remember how we
took selfies with Obama's cardboard cutout?

Gun Ghazal

I am a fan of water pistols but an enemy of guns;
pull out those Super Soakers and put away those big guns.

My boyfriend tried to teach me how to shoot a target:
goggles on, ears plugged, arms extended, I had just begun

my period, and all I could think of was blood, the good kind,
my body busy and alive—slick with its own potential. I let the gun

go slack in my hand. "Is this a deal-breaker?" he asked. It was.
The same boyfriend used to kiss his biceps and call them "guns."

A Vietnam War protester placed a carnation in a rifle's barrel.
Once, years before, Mae West ribbed a police officer: "Is that a gun

in your pocket...?" My father loved Matt Dillon on *Gunsmoke*;
when my parents fought, my mother called me their "smoking gun."

My mother was afraid of her own temper. No pistols for her—
instead, scrubbing floors and pounding meatloaves, then gunning

the gas and leaning on the horn. I'm afraid of my temper too.
I'm afraid of leading with anger, like feudal lords and shoguns,

so certain they were right. I'd rather punch my pillow than
reach for a weapon. As Chekhov warned, when there's a gun

in your story, someone has to pull the trigger. That's why
we love or fear them. Shooting is the only purpose of a gun.

Masked Ghazal

Now that we know we have to wear them, we choose fun masks—
in Florida, flamingos, gators, scuba fins and snorkel masks.

For Barbra, the cat lover, a calico print with whiskers;
for Margot, the Shakespeare scholar, "roses damask'd,"

tie-dyed floral patterns across her own cheeks. For John,
a Lone Ranger mask disguising his eyes, and a silver mask

with glitter for the pandemic bride. Even emojis cover
some, like facial mood rings. Self-expression while masked

is easy—SCIENCE, VOTE, LOVE—though our smiles
are hidden. Tears are harder to hide. Goggles, masks

for the eyes, fog up, make life blurry. And face visors
must get plenty of solar and fluorescent glare. Any mask

is a poet's friend, a way into the other as well as the self.
Speaker. Persona. Third person. The metaphor in masks

is endless fun: Lady Lazarus, My Last Duchess,
Daffy Duck in Hollywood. Colette wrote of masks

to heighten sensual pleasure, hiding and revealing,
the body shrouded at first, then slowly unmasked...

What is under the U.S.? What will be disclosed
when we lift at last our nation's sock-and-buskin masks?

Zoom Ghazal

Sometimes the days pass so quickly—zoom!
Sometimes the days pass so slowly on Zoom

where colleagues seem tiny in their chairs,
heads perfectly squishable now. Kids Zoom

and learn the alphabet without a teacher's hand
scrawling on a board: *A is for absent, Z is for Zoom.*

We celebrate cyber birthdays, cry at #zoomerals,
grow nostalgic at Mazda commercials (*Zoom-Zoom*),

thinking of the cancelled road trips and plane trips.
Remember zipping across Alligator Alley, zooming

maskless, dirty hands on the wheel? Stopping for gas
a mindless chore of the touch-and-go Before. Zoom

in on our shared bucket of popcorn, fingers scooping
the hot buttery florets as our elbows touch. Zoom

out, and there's a movie on a big screen, strangers around
a crowded buffet. TV dinners are to potlucks as Zoom

karaoke singers are to packed dance floors. I once took a sip
from someone else's punch—no biggie then. Zoom

went my cheeks, and soon I was dizzy, delightedly spiked.
Tonight I toss, counting my Zzzzzs. Dream-screen. Dream-Zoom.

Ruth Bader Ginsburg Ghazal

(March 15, 1933–September 18, 2020)

When RBG wore her silver "dissenting" collar,
she must've been hot under the collar.

Would men ever take their feet off her neck
or just expect she'd rinse the ring around her collar?

Can she still see us now that she's passed,
through the murky glass ceiling, an opaque pink collar?

A Hollywood movie and documentary memorialize
her courage and landmark cases, why we call her

notorious, buy RBG T-shirts, stickers, and face masks,
why little girls trick-or-treat in her signature lace collar.

VMI, Obergefell v. Hodges, Sessions v. Dimaya:
She met some haters among the hetero white-collars,

like *The NY Post* who characterized her as Darth Bader,
the cartoonists who drew her in a bulldog's spiked collar.

But RGB laughed it off, and when Kate McKinnon
played her on *SNL*, bespectacled and collared,

working out—teabag punching bags, Q-tip barbells—
she might have been the wake-up caller

we ignored. Surely, we thought, she'd live forever:
Now SCOTUS is her cenotaph, a gaping shock collar.

Give-and-Take Ghazal

I would like to give more than I take
in this world of takers. I forgive

others for being snippy or falling short,
then blame myself when I mistake

tolerance for interest. It's hard to be humored
and still be gracious. My smile gives

away my misgivings, yet frowning feels
like I'm auditioning. Here are the outtakes

of my outreach: forced laughter and awkward
nods of the head. Give me a break, give

me a hug—but don't: it's the era of social distance
and curbside pick-up and take-out. Take

your time, but don't leave me waiting too long.
Come on, democracy. Give me liberty, or give

me a free lunch with sushi rolls, sashimi,
and seaweed salad. Take my advice—take

a breather (when was your last deep breath?),
then exhale as slow as you can. Give in, give

out or away, but not up. Never *up*. Enduring is
giving it your all, taking your time to take.

Helen Reddy Ghazal

(October 25, 1941- September 29, 2020)

In 1971, women were ready to roar.
In 2021, will women be able to roar

like their grandmothers, jazzy flappers
and suffragists whose vote was their roar?

What will these new Roaring Twenties bring?
After four years of hisses and whimpers, roars

of laughter or angry howls at the ballot box?
Hashtag feminism and Katy Perry's "Roar"

as we Zumba on Zoom, jitterbug on TikTok—
part MTM kitten and part MGM roar.

A lion's mane under each armpit, Lourdes Leon
treads stealthily around spotlights, her roar

less pronounced than her mother's. O, mothers,
in numbers too big to ignore, may your uproar—

working from home, kids on iPads, virtual school—
strike like a tidal wave at the polls, a mighty roar

from the oceans of your throats. Every Helen
a light in the harbor, a novice no longer, aroar

in her power, rips off the faded rose of days gone by.
No flowers or lullabies now, just her eleventh-hour roar!

This is Not a Test Ghazal

Voters for Hillary saw in their Rorschach test
an eerie glimmer of standard achievement tests

on which A+ girls scored lower than B- boys.
These capable full-grown women could attest

to being labeled *shrill, cute, bitchy, ballbuster,*
their placement tests switched out for purity tests,

screen tests, fill-in-the-blank quizzes, breast exams.
Even a female Secretary of State might be tested

for her knowledge of cookie recipes, judged
as if competing in a Miss Congeniality contest.

Then we studied ourselves—what had we done
to embody yearbook superlatives like *Quietest,*

Most Likely to Give In, Most Likely Not to Complain.
When did *loneliest* become a synonym for *smartest,*

ambitious become a synonym for *pushy, loud?*
A single factor is always decisive on a litmus test.

Will she laugh at my jokes? Or is she the jokester?
Should she smile pretty at the proctor she detests?

Never ham it up, never wear all your jewels at once.
What happens next is not the end—it's just the latest.

Truth-or-Dare Ghazal

Now a nation of post-truth and post-D.A.R.E.,
our Prez and his son snort lines of "truth,"

then chase them with hydroxychloroquine cocktails.
They tweet conspiracies, wondering if Americans dare

question their hoodwinks and humdingers. Maybe sobriety is
letting go of what we can't control. Maybe the truth

was always a tail we chased, but now the whole
kite's torn, stuck in a tree. Dr. Kildare,

a fictional medical doctor, could find work on TV,
but the Prez stifles real Dr. Fauci. "The truth

will set you free, but first, it will piss you off,"
said Gloria. At the Women's March she dared

women to put their bodies where their beliefs are
and be shrill, feisty, unafraid to speak the truth;

in a gruesome parody, the Prez now urges
Proud Boys to be shrill, issues a double-dog-dare

to "poll-watchers" and populists everywhere.
Anna Julia Cooper, Ida Bell Wells, Sojourner Truth,

forerunners of Black Lives Matter, foremothers of
NOW, fought the devils. Let's be angels who dare.

Trick-or-Treat Ghazal

Trompe l'oeil is many painters' favorite trick—
a pear that looks so real you want to treat

yourself to a bite. I prefer plums actually,
cold from the fridge, a WCW trick

where a Post-it note becomes a poem
anthologized to the point students treat

it as parody, not art. E. Bishop wrote
"One Art" about loss, how the trick

is learning to "master" grief before
the last stanza, before you retreat

into permanent sorrow. The plum
dumplings your grammy made tricked

you into liking prunes, the shriveled heart
you'd one day grow after a man mistreated

you. How he mocked your "pear shape"
and hid the Halloween candy to trick

you into abstaining. No sweets for the
kids either. Our *Trump l'oeil* President entreats

us to nibble the carrot he dangles, as if
the carrot were real and not another orange trick.

General Election Ghazal

November 3, 2020

All day this bruised feeling in this purple state
of McMansions and trailer parks, real estate

moguls and ne'er-do-wells. Florida, I fear,
will always wind up blood red, a hateful state,

sidewinder of the Southeast. Hiss and rattle
of voter suppression, a one-way swing state

that has never been true blue—only ever powder.
What is the state of our union, the state

of each little white star? Are they asterisks now
on a white power flag? Is it too obvious to state

that we *are* divisible, that liberty and justice
are for the wealthy, Roosevelt's welfare state

footnoted **Results not typical. Exceptions apply.*
We agreed to have felons' voting rights reinstated,

yet they are mired down in our red state red tape
which favors bluer eyes. The Sunshine State—

67 counties on a jacquard election map,
a penis-shaped puzzle with an enlarged prostate—

tonight's just another flaccid disappointment
in which the state of democracy lies in state.

Counting Ghazal

I have counted to ten, counted sheep, counted
coffee beans and magic beans to avoid counting

the electoral college map, its arcane pathways
to victory and defeat. Meanwhile, the body count

keeps rising, Covid-19 deaths and killings by police.
No resurrection for the lost lives, no recount

of bullets. No refunds on body bags or funeral costs,
the pricey lilies and pinwheel sandwiches. No discount

on hurricane supplies or wildfire evacuation kits.
Like a hot new reality show, promos for *THE COUNT*

keep me hooked on cable. Percentages in blue districts
a slow-rising tide. Crowds chant the obvious: "Count!"

or "Stop the count!" depending on their candidate
of choice. I watch, discountenanced. Now I see the *count*

in Count Chocula, that counterculture cereal vampire,
cartoon parody of a much more sinister Count

who preferred drinking blood and impaling noblemen.
How allegorical! I see the *count* in country too: who counts

in this countdown. We tell the poor to count their blessings,
while the corrupt elites are never called to account.

Wellness Ghazal

November 7, 2020

When every email begins "I hope you are well,"
you know that everyone is tentative to dwell

in possibility, the way Dickinson said we must.
I threw all my change into a wishing well.

I downloaded a meditation app but fell asleep
to a nightmare of dry pens and spilled inkwells.

In dreams, I forget my mask, my voting precinct.
Awake, I obsess about Trump, our ne'er-do-well

Democratic Party. Is the donkey mascot more apt
with its kicks? I add them to my workouts. Farewell,

loose skin! I'm so tense my leg cramps can't be cured
by the quinine in seltzer. I watch my fingers swell,

then wrap my hands and punch the heavy bag so hard
my knuckles are purple mountain majesties. Oh well,

my amber waves are actually gray, and spacious skies
are graying too. I grab my umbrella, run down the stairwell,

out toward the sea. The salty air still soothes me—
its ancient curative powers. I put down my beach towel

and stretch out in the intermittent sun. Despite the wind,
Joe and Kamala have won. For now, all's well that ends well.

Jeopardy! Ghazal

(Alex Trebek, July 22, 1940 – November 8, 2020)

What are an elegy and a eulogy, Alex?
What are the five stages of grief, Alex?

Did you know Elizabeth Kubler-Ross, Alex?
How will America stay smart now, Alex?

Did you ever wish you'd stayed in Canada, Alex?
Did you ever wish you'd stuck to journalism, Alex?

What was your favorite answer you ever gave, Alex?
Is it true you had a 143 IQ, Alex?

Did you hire a ghost-writer for your memoir, Alex?
Did you ever dream of writing poetry instead, Alex?

What are a requiem and an obituary, Alex?
Was Lucille Ball a good friend, Alex?

Did you cast your last vote for Joe Biden, Alex?
Did you ever guess the U.S. was in jeopardy, Alex?

What will you miss most about this world, Alex?
How many children have been named after you, Alex?

Did you have a favorite contestant, Alex?
Did you have a favorite candy bar, Alex?

What can't the audience tell about the host, Alex?
What will we never know, Alex?

Fraud Ghazal

When the President-Reject claims voter fraud,
it's a classic case of the fraud calling the fair fraud.

You don't need to have studied Sigmund Freud
to recognize his denial with intent to defraud

supporters who hope to be just like him. A fake
out, a foul ball, a fictive narrative—fraud

alerts after he steals your credit cards,
fire alarm after he burns your house down. Fraud

President, Fraud Fürer, Furious Grifter,
Felonious Debtor, ever uncouth and unkind. Defraud

efforts include the unlawful "legal" funds to fight
ballot-counting in five states; 45 have called fraud

on 45! He repeats lies until he believes them.
Even Fox News grows wary of the Human Fraud,

while hosts try to cajole him into conceding:
Defraud us once, shame on us! Zoom in. But defraud

us twice? Sir, does that mean you're a cult leader?
Pan out. Should the Bamboozled revolt, the Fraud

Sociopath will be exposed at last. We wait
for a Fraudian slip, the final indictment for Freud.

Transition Ghazal

So much for a peaceful transition;
I'd settle for even a puerile transition.

Every time I squirt Purell, I blame him,
this Unconceder, blocking Biden's transition.

When will he go, this Lame Duck L'Orange?
He who won't listen can't possibly transition.

Tasteless jokes already have begun—Caitlyn
Jenner made a much smoother transition.

For example, after, before, henceforth,
during, heretofore: movement fuels transition.

In pre-K, teachers play music between lessons.
The child who doesn't find a chair must transition

to standing up, losing the game with grace.
Tantrums at four—an expected part of transition.

Tantrums at 74? He bullies, and the bullied
beg for more. I fear the oxymoron "cyclical transition"—

will he leave and then come back, a revolving door
of fake news and manufactured rage? Transition

from democracy to what exactly? Trump's coup
du jour is our lost faith in a peaceful transition.

Future Ghazal

I try to stay present, but I flash to the future:
no flying cars or floating homes like a *Jetsons* future;

instead, sinkholes and fires and underwater streets.
Our Rosies are sent to Robot Detention Centers in a future

of fembots and handmaids—the patriarchy gasping
on a stolen ventilator, still weighing its options and futures.

"The Global Seed Bank flooded" sounds like the punchline
 to an international sperm bank joke. Future

generations might never taste a real banana,
might never see bees pollinating poppies. The future

might be foraging and lots of walking, no cars,
no quibbling about gas prices. Even a Prius isn't future-

friendly, but it could serve as a place to sleep
if we who teach Humanities prove expendable. Futures

for Frontliners worked for a while, free community college
for high-demand careers. The FFA, once the Future

Farmers of America, became the Fucked Farmers whose soil
is eroding, crops degrading. Remember in *Back to the Future*

how Marty takes his own mother to prom? The past
just a strange romance, until the last dance of the future.

Dolly Parton Ghazal

When I was a kid, I thought they made *Hello, Dolly!*
about you. You dreamt the Hollywood sign read "Dolly-

wood," and one day it did in East Tennessee! "Dolly's
Imagination Library," a $35 custom license plate Dolly

fans in the Volunteer State can purchase as of 2016. Dolly,
an avid reader, you give books to TN children. Dolly,

you knew how books keep on giving, unlike Slinkys and dollies.
Each move I'd box my poetry volumes and roll them on a dolly

up the U-Haul ramp. The best books last forever, as you must, Dolly—
bringing together cowboys and drag queens dressed as Dolly,

Appalachian Pride and LGBTQ Pride side by side. Dolly,
how many have chosen you as a write-in candidate? *Dolly*

Parton for President! Jane Fonda as your running mate? Oh, Dolly,
how you sparkle, star-spangled and wise as the Dalai

Lama. You have been my spiritual leader, Dolly.
I prayed to your tiny waist as I gobbled Hostess and Dolly

Madison cakes, to your big wigs as my hair thinned, Dolly.
Your authenticity fluttered fake eyelashes, Dolly,

and I wanted to see the world as you saw it. Dolly,
I feel the room swayin'. Promise you'll never go away, Dolly.

Forward Ghazal

Now that the country can at last move forward,
as the verso page turns toward the foreword,

I read whole sentences without distraction.
I highlight passages that seem especially forward-

thinking in Rutger Bregman's *Utopia for Realists*.
Four years ago, hope froze in me. Fast-forward,

and today, I begin to thaw. I'm still afraid to hope
for quick fixes, but at last we have a straightforward

President-Elect and the first woman Vice President.
Meanwhile, the President-Reject does not pay it forward,

and memes abound, including "Anita Recount"
and "Bye Don." Some of us are simply lost for words.

We beep car horns and cry into our masks.
We set countdown clocks till we can spring forward

to an extra hour of metaphorical daylight.
Meanwhile, the President-Reject spews four words:

"Widespread fraud. Stand by." *You're Fired!* signs
sprout on lawns and screens alike. Going forward,

I hope there are no more tell-alls, no more NDAs,
just a peaceful ethos and a vision truly planet-forward.

Meta Ghazal

I always wanted to write a ghazal
once I learned to pronounce it: *guzzle*.

All week the trees have guzzled rain—
repetitive storms like end words in a ghazal.

An uneasy susurrus accompanies this rain,
the whirlwind of potential Hurricane Gisel.

In *sturm und drang*, my thirst for beauty grows,
my thirst for repetition—nuzzle, puzzle, ghazal.

Palm fronds in the road, pelicans in the sky—
the opposite of the desert where a gazelle

makes graceful haste across an arid plain.
Agha Shahid Ali introduced me to the ghazal:

"he has bought grief's lottery, bought even the rain."
More recently, Marilyn Hacker writes political ghazals,

probes how we each contribute to "the dark times."
Some of us bite our fingernails; some guzzle

beer, climb trees, feed birds, or play the lottery.
Others rewrite scary fairy tales—Hansel and Ghazal,

Rumplesonnet, Cindervillanelle. Our poem-thirst
to make sense of the world—a sip, then a ghazal.

Acknowledgments

Grateful acknowledgment is made to the editors and staff members of the magazines in which poems from *The Latest* first appeared:

Court Green: "Gun Ghazal," "Ruth Bader Ginsburg Ghazal," "This Is Not a Test Ghazal," "Truth-or-Dare Ghazal," and "Meta Ghazal."

Rattle: "Give-and-Take Ghazal."

Smartish Pace: "Future Ghazal."

Swamp Ape: "Trick-or-Treat Ghazal" and "Fraud Ghazal."

"Dolly Parton Ghazal" appeared in *Let Me Say This: A Dolly Parton Poetry Anthology* (edited by Julie E. Bloemeke & Dustin Brookshire), Madville Press, 2023.

Denise Duhamel's most recent books of poetry are *Pink Lady* (Pitt Poetry Series, 2025), *Second Story* (2021), and *Scald* (2017). *Blowout* (2013) was a finalist for the National Book Critics Circle Award. *In Which* (2024) is a winner of the Rattle Chapbook Prize. She and the late Maureen Seaton co-authored five collections, the most recent of which was *CAPRICE: Collaborations Collected, Uncollected, and New* (Sibling Rivalry Press, 2015). A recipient of fellowships from the Guggenheim Foundation and the National Endowment for the Arts, she is a distinguished university professor in the MFA program at Florida International University in Miami.

Julie Marie Wade is the author of many collections of poetry, prose, and hybrid forms, most recently *Quick Change Artist: Poems* (Anhinga Press, 2025), selected by Octavio Quintanilla as the winner of the 2023 Anhinga Prize in Poetry and *The Mary Years* (Texas Review Press, 2024), selected by Michael Martone as the winner of the 2023 Clay Reynolds Novella Prize. A recipient of the Lambda Literary Award for Lesbian Memoir and grants from the Kentucky Arts Council and the Barbara Deming Memorial Fund, Wade makes her home with Angie Griffin and their two cats in Dania Beach and is a professor in the MFA program at Florida International University in Miami.

Denise Duhamel & Julie Marie Wade have been writing together since 2014. Their co-authored poems and essays have appeared in *Arts & Letters, Bellingham Review, The Biscayne Times, Cincinnati Review, The Common, Five Points, Fourth Genre, The Kenyon Review, The Los Angeles Review, The Louisville Review, The Normal School, Painted Bride Quarterly, Passages North, The Pinch, South Dakota Review,* and *Tupelo Quarterly*, among other literary journals and anthologies. In 2017, they received the Glenna Luschei Prize from *Prairie Schooner* for their collaborative essay, "13 Superstitions," and in 2019, their first collection of essays, *The Unrhymables: Collaborations in Prose,* was published by Noctuary Press.

About Small Harbor Publishing

Small Harbor Publishing is a 501c3 nonprofit organization. Our goal is to publish unique and diverse voices. We are a feminist press, and we are committed to diversity and inclusion. We strive to bring new voices to a devoted and expanding readership.

Small Harbor Publishing began in 2018 with the first issue of *Harbor Review*. The magazine is an online space where poetry and art converse. *Harbor Review* quickly grew and now publishes reviews and runs multiple micro chapbook competitions, including the Washburn Prize and the Editor's Prize.

In July 2020, Small Harbor Publishing was officially incorporated and began Harbor Editions. Harbor Editions accepts submissions through a chapbook open reading period, a hybrid chapbook open reading period, the Marginalia Series, and the Laureate Prize.

In 2023, Harbor Anthologies began with a mission to promote texts that explore social justice issues and highlight marginalized writers.

If you would like to support Small Harbor Publishing, visit our "About" page at: smallharborpublishing.com/about.